Thoughts That Empower

*Inspiring Thoughts to Help You
Navigate Life's Journey*

Fred T. Williams

ISBN: 0-6925978-2-4
ISBN-13: 978-0-692-59782-8

For more information, to book an event, or to book Fred for an event, visit www.fredtwilliams.com or email officialfredtwilliams@gmail.com.

Printed in the United States of America.

ALSO BY FRED T. WILLIAMS

The Path Away From There

I Hope This Helps Along The Way

DEDICATION

This book is dedicated to the first woman I ever loved, my mother, the late Alberta Williams.

You taught me how to love God, love people and embrace life. You saw greatness in me and made sure that I knew you did. I learned to believe in myself because of you. There isn't a day that goes by that I don't miss you, or think about the many sacrifices you made to raise my brother and I. In our very last conversation, you made me promise you that when I die the world would have known that I lived. You challenged me to leave my mark. I pray that I am making you proud.

CONTENTS

INTRODUCTION

As a child I was the one who always asked the question "why". The way things work and what made a person tick was and continues to be something very interesting to me. All of my life I have been in the "people business". Whether it's from the dynamic of ministry within the church or from laboring to help people maximize their life holistically, knowing how people think and process is a very important part of what I do.

In my study of people, I have found out that so many of the problems we face have very much to do with how we think. If we are crippled in our thinking or we are damaged in the way we process our thoughts, it directly affects the quality of our decisions, which stifle the productivity of our lives. I have seen this time and time again. At one point in my life I had to confront this issue within myself.

These collection of thoughts are written simply to behoove you to think about your life, your purpose, how you view and handle love, and the relationships you have. May these thoughts from the lessons I've learned along the way inspire and empower each reader to becoming better and achieving greater.

Thoughts On
LIFE & PURPOSE

THOUGHT

1

*"When you know who you are
everything else is truly
background noise."*

THOUGHT

2

"Your actions are the evidence of the truth of your word. If your actions don't match what you say, your word means nothing."

<u>THOUGHT</u>

3

"You can give a person an opportunity for better, but if their character and discipline doesn't line up, it will ruin things quickly."

THOUGHT

4

"Don't let your fight against mediocrity cause you to abuse the relationships that God sent in your life to give you favor and to change your life."

THOUGHT

5

"Sometimes you are the very reason why your gift will never make it to center stage and work on your behalf. The gift is nothing without the character to match."

THOUGHT

6

"You will realize why no one wanted to help some people, just make sure you don't realize too late."

THOUGHT

7

"You don't get to call shots if you haven't made the sacrifice. Sacrifice is not just giving your time to something, but it's giving your substance!"

THOUGHT

8

"Never argue with people who hope you fail."

<u>THOUGHT</u>

9

"You can't push people higher that keep dragging you lower."

THOUGHT

10

"Sometimes you have to stop hiding how gifted you really are behind how gifted some people think they are."

THOUGHT

11

"Never be afraid to be who you are out of the fear of what others will think or say. You being you will free others to be who they are."

THOUGHT

12

"Your hustle must match your dream. If it doesn't, don't be upset with anyone but yourself. Either step up your hustle or get a new dream. Simple."

THOUGHT

13

"Manage your expectations and you can minimize your disappointments."

THOUGHT

14

"A person's actions help you gauge what to expect from them. You can expect more, but don't be upset when you don't get it. After all, people can only be who they are."

THOUGHT

15

"Never let who you were stop you from becoming who you were meant to be."

THOUGHT

16

"Defeat is not an option and losing is unacceptable. Play to win or don't play at all!"

THOUGHT

17

"You want everyone to win with you, but the only ones that can win with you are the ones who have the heart and stamina to run with you."

THOUGHT

18

"Life doesn't come with an eraser, but it does come with a red pen. The red pen doesn't erase but it helps bring clarity. Even though you can't undo the things that have been done, you can red line them and make notations to ensure your story reads correctly."

<u>THOUGHT</u>

19

"No matter what happens...don't stop moving forward."

THOUGHT

20

"The failures of my life have prompted my greatest successes."

THOUGHT

21

"No one looks back on their life and remembers the nights they had plenty of sleep."

THOUGHT

22

"Don't be guilty of being present in everyone else's life but absent in your own."

THOUGHT

23

"The best way to silence your critics is to keep moving as if their voice or opinion doesn't matter. Truth is it really doesn't."

THOUGHT

24

"It's not the people who make it clear that they don't like you that you have to be concerned about. It's the ones that say they love you, comment on your social media posts, and try to actually get you to open up to them while they look for a chink in your armor and are hoping you fail."

THOUGHT

25

"Focusing on the pain can rob you of the joy in receiving the promise."

THOUGHT

26

"All you need is a glimpse of your tomorrow to get you through the hell of your today."

THOUGHT

27

"Don't let your life be one long run-on sentence. You need to put some periods in there somewhere, and maybe an exclamation point every now and then just to keep things clear."

THOUGHT

28

"Having a dream is like having a God's eye view of your destination but not knowing the path to get there. As long as you keep the destination in mind, the path to get there won't be able to make you quit no matter how tough it may be."

THOUGHT

29

"You have to believe in the impossible to see the unexplainable."

THOUGHT

30

"Don't let fear paralyze you in what faith is trying to propel you through."

THOUGHT

31

"Success doesn't make itself. It's the product of smart work and consistent grind. So rise and grind!"

THOUGHT

32

"It didn't come from God if you had to create fake pay-stubs with an exaggerated income, lie on the application, practice any sort of deceit, or you stepped on someone to get it. Often times what we get as a result of these type of actions is testified about as a "blessing" from God when in actuality they are curses you've attached to yourself. If you had to lie to get it you will have to lie to keep it. And you can't satisfy God by living a lie. The things that come as a result of lies only last for so long. Pleasing God requires honesty."

THOUGHT

33

"Having integrity is not about what you do in public, but rather about everything you do in private."

THOUGHT

34

"God will not use a man or woman whom He cannot hold accountable."

THOUGHT

35

"Who you are and what you'll be is determined by what and how you think."

THOUGHT

36

"You will never face a challenge that God hasn't given you the strength to overcome."

<u>THOUGHT</u>

37

"Stay focused and let nothing and no one distract you. One moment of distraction can cost you everything."

THOUGHT

38

"It is not noble to not do the wrong that you desire to do. The issue to deal with is why you desire to do it in the first place. At some point you will have to deal with your desires or your desires will deal with you."

THOUGHT

39

*"You will have whatever you say.
What are you saying?"*

THOUGHT

40

"We all have the same 24 hours in the day to do something that will make us better and that will make us great. What are you doing with the time you have?"

THOUGHT

41

"Help isn't help unless it's the help that you need. Eliminate your circle of people who keep trying to help you the way they want instead of the way you need."

THOUGHT

42

"Each week should begin with a declaration of purpose, a plan for productivity and a hustle that produces results. Success favors the prepared."

THOUGHT

43

"You have to be willing to do what you know you've been called to do the way you know you've been called to do it, regardless of how unpopular it may be. Every trailblazer was once called crazy and was told what they were doing wouldn't work. But they did it anyway. Don't just walk the path; blaze the trail!"

THOUGHT

44

"You have to be consistent in your character. Don't be honest in the morning and a liar in the evening. The inconsistency of your character could very well be the reason for the inconsistency in your life."

THOUGHT

45

"Don't let the expectations of others outweigh the expectations you put on yourself. Challenge yourself to be better. Push yourself to be greater."

THOUGHT

46

"Since people are going to talk about you anyway, it only makes sense to live a life that's worth their mention."

THOUGHT

47

"Don't plan yourself out of God's plans for you."

THOUGHT

48

"People will try to make you feel guilty for achieving the things they didn't have the gift, skill or discipline to. You don't owe anyone an explanation of your grind; and you definitely don't owe anyone an apology for your success."

THOUGHT

49

"Never let people who aren't going anywhere stop you from going somewhere."

THOUGHT

50

"Only give your time and attention to the people, places and things that matter. Doing other than that can cost you your sanity."

THOUGHT

51

"Social media and text messaging has given way for a generation full of "thumb thugs". They are huge behind a keyboard but can't bust a grape in real life."

THOUGHT

52

"To be in the flow of destiny you have to be willing to leave the shores of mediocrity, and you must be bold and daring enough to sail your boat of faith across the stormy sea of doubt."

THOUGHT

53

"The best advertisement for your brand is you. If you don't believe in what you represent why should others?"

THOUGHT

54

"Command your week to be a success. Command your week to be productive. Command your week to bring you into the flow of destiny. You will have whatever you say."

THOUGHT

55

"How you view failing will ultimately determine how it affects you. You can fail and learn, allowing that failure to push you to a win; or you can fail and be bitter, allowing that failure to make you a failure. It's all about your perspective. Just because you fail at something doesn't mean you're a failure. Remember, success is birth out of a series of failures."

THOUGHT

56

"Find what you're good at and do it! It doesn't have to be music and sports. Whatever it is, find it and then find a way to make money doing it!"

THOUGHT

57

"Even though it's easy to always point out what's wrong, condition yourself to focus on everything that's right. What you focus on the most will determine what you see the most of. If all you see is wrong then everything will always be wrong. But if you focus on what's right, you will be able to look at what's wrong and figure out how to make it right."

THOUGHT

58

"We often get frustrated in life because we're having the right conversations with wrong people or we're having the wrong conversations with the right people. Know who is who in your life and make sure you are having the right conversations with the right people."

THOUGHT

59

"If you learn to properly manage yourself you will be able to properly manage what you have. You cannot expect to handle things the right way when you handle yourself the wrong way."

THOUGHT

60

"You should always plan for the unexpected. Just because you don't expect it doesn't mean you shouldn't be prepared for it. Prevention is always better than a cure."

THOUGHT

61

"The things that don't matter in life only matter if you allow them to. Choose to leave the unimportant where it is."

THOUGHT

62

"Impersonators and copycats are never remembered...only originals. Be original."

THOUGHT

63

"For some, rough seasons are a prison; and like prisoners who have been institutionalized find it hard to make it in the real world, some people allow their rough seasons to make it hard for them to live in the good season that come their way. It's the cycle of life. There are good seasons and there are rough seasons. Each season is necessary and critical to having balance. The key is living in the rough seasons while holding onto the hope of the good ones. Don't let your rough seasons make you bitter or afraid. Let them make you better and fearless! And always remember...seasons change."

THOUGHT

64

"Sometimes your deepest thought can be your greatest fault. You don't handle a treasure like you can just find it anywhere. Don't let your mind get you in trouble by missing what's right here because you're busy trying to see what's over there."

THOUGHT

65

"There's power in knowing what to lend your words to. Not everything warrants a response."

THOUGHT

66

"The depth of our consecration will determine the intensity through which the power of God flows through us. The more of us we empty out, the more of Him we can take in."

THOUGHT

67

"It is impossible to expect God to move in a situation you have not even made room for Him in. When you take your hands off of it, then He can put His hand on it."

THOUGHT

68

"You can only have the life you dream when you learn to not get too caught up in the life you have. The hardest thing to do is to let go. Don't hold the life you have so tight that you unknowingly swat away the life you've dreamed about."

THOUGHT

69

"Everyone you need to know is not somebody that everyone knows. Simply put, don't mishandle who you assume is a 'nobody' simply because everyone doesn't know them just yet. You could be mishandling the next leading voice of a generation."

THOUGHT

70

"If I had a penny for some people's thoughts, a penny is all I would have. If the way you think hasn't changed your life for the better do you actually believe it would add value to anyone else?"

THOUGHT

71

"Between 11pm and 3am is when people do a lot of things that they regret. Don't let your midnight musings cost you your integrity."

THOUGHT

72

"You have to release some things in order to receive some things. Don't miss your chance to get what you need because you aren't willing to let go of what you don't need."

THOUGHT

73

"I used to want to press rewind and undo all of the bad times in my life; but then I realized that the best parts of me were developed in those bad times. I am good because those times were bad."

THOUGHT

74

"Don't run from the quiet, but don't let it consume you either. The quiet can be the best place to find balance between your thoughts, but it can also be a prison if you stay too long."

THOUGHT

75

"It's what you do with what you have that will determine what you get, how much you get, and when you'll get it. Work what you have, and watch what you get!"

THOUGHT

76

"They were never for you if their support of you stopped when you started walking in your purpose and not their wishes."

THOUGHT

77

"Every leap of faith begins with a small step of focus."

THOUGHT

78

"If you don't care about the integrity of your name, why should others?"

THOUGHT

79

"You can either complain about everything that is going wrong or you can maximize on all that's going right."

THOUGHT

80

"The best thing to do is fail at never trying."

THOUGHT

81

"Never apologize for being true."

THOUGHT

82

"Challenge yourself to be better. Don't be afraid to set a standard for yourself that you have to live up to. After all, you cannot expect others to respect you if you don't respect yourself."

THOUGHT

83

"A renewed mind will allow you to face the same obstacles with a fresh perspective. Your perspective can either pin you in prison or propel you in purpose."

THOUGHT

84

"Loving God is about embracing His plan for your life. You cannot love Him but hate His plan."

THOUGHT

85

"The simplest things done with the purest heart can have the greatest impact."

THOUGHT

86

"Almost everyone has sight, but how many of us actually have vision?"

THOUGHT

87

"When you are in God's flow for your life you don't have to make anything happen. You just have to walk down the path He's designed and see what's already happened. Your submission to His lead lets you see what He sees."

THOUGHT

88

"You must deal with the internal conflict so that you can correct the outward dysfunction."

THOUGHT

89

"Never mistake a good idea for a God-idea. God ideas are always with someone else in mind. We just happen to benefit from them."

THOUGHT

90

"Desires determine dreams.
Change your desires and you can
change your dreams."

THOUGHT

91

"Don't be so caught up in those who clap for you, but be grateful for those that stand with you."

THOUGHT

92

"When you know who and what you are, it doesn't matter who tells you who and what you are not."

THOUGHT

93

"Never spend more time talking about your vision that you don't spend enough time working your vision."

THOUGHT

94

"You will never get back time wasted; but time wisely invested will always yield a great return."

THOUGHT

95

"No matter what happens, never be guilty of being the one to assault the character of people. Truth is you are always a misstep away from a fall yourself."

THOUGHT

96

"You cannot go through life simply receiving and never giving. Nor can you go through life giving and never receiving. There has to be a balance between the two."

THOUGHT

97

"Be determined to be the difference and not get lost in the status quo."

THOUGHT

98

"Learn to respond only to that which is worthy of a response. Your attention is priceless so you shouldn't just give it to anything and anyone."

THOUGHT

99

"There is nothing more fulfilling than knowing that you are living in purpose on purpose. Never confuse living out the plans of people with living out the purpose of God."

THOUGHT

100

"Prioritize your life and don't worry about who feels what way about the order you set. Don't kill yourself for the sake of anyone. You are good to no one dead."

THOUGHT

101

"The way you live today will determine the joy you walk in tomorrow."

THOUGHT

102

"Don't let the TV and/or society tell you who and what to be."

THOUGHT

103

"You can choose to exist or you can dare to live.

THOUGHT

104

"If you want to be remembered be different."

THOUGHT

105

"Complaining about every bad day could be the very reason why you haven't experienced any good days."

THOUGHT

106

"The quality of your life is a result of the quality of your choices."

THOUGHT

107

"Insecure people ALWAYS scream the loudest."

THOUGHT

108

"Don't give up ownership of your dream by allowing others to outwork you in seeing it come to pass."

THOUGHT

109

"It takes more energy to be negative than it does to be positive. Negativity drains you while positivity rejuvenates you."

THOUGHT

110

"Be careful talking to stupid people. Their stupidity will have you thinking you're crazy."

THOUGHT

111

"Scream instead of whisper, run instead of walk, and laugh instead of cry. Do something different to see something different."

THOUGHT

112

"Ladies, be like the woman who gets paid with her clothes on, instead of the woman who is paid for the clothes she takes off."

THOUGHT

113

"Tell yourself what God promised you loud enough for your echo to remind you.

THOUGHT

114

"Dreams are free to have but costly to live. If you want to live the dream then you have to pay for it."

THOUGHT

115

"Don't be so boastful about your clean hands that you ignore your filthy heart."

THOUGHT

116

"A true champion trains in the off season. Just because it's not your time doesn't mean you can't be prepared."

THOUGHT

117

"We always look for the "yes" to give us what we want when it's the "no" that saves our lives."

THOUGHT

118

"Do everything you do from the heart and it's guaranteed to touch someone's heart."

THOUGHT

119

"How well you dance in the bad times will determine how long the good times last."

THOUGHT

120

"You will never experience freedom until you learn to love the truth. It is the truth that comes and constructs freedom in your life."

THOUGHT

121

"The reason why you feel like you keep going in circles could be because you refused the help of the people who knew how to advance you for the assistance of the ones trying to figure it out. Help really isn't help unless it's the help that you need."

THOUGHT

122

"Average is never remembered; above average gets honorable mention; but greatness defines history. "

THOUGHT

123

"If what happened to you had the power to kill you, you wouldn't be reading this."

THOUGHT

124

"What has value to you is what you make time for. If you want to know what you value, examine what gets your time."

THOUGHT

125

"Refuse to compromise to be popular with man. Maintain your standard with God and let Him handle your audience."

THOUGHT

126

"Everyone that's in your face and in your ear does not have you in their heart."

THOUGHT

127

"Never build a bridge to your yesterday when your yesterday almost cost you your today. Burn the bridge."

THOUGHT

128

"We don't just read history, but every day we write it."

THOUGHT

129

"Every day should be a faith walk filled with calculated efforts that you depend on God to pull together to paint a masterpiece for His glory."

THOUGHT

130

"Let go of anything that hinders Him (God) from having and using all of you."

THOUGHT

131

"Sometimes you do qualify for what you don't qualify for."

THOUGHT

132

"Courage invites critics."

THOUGHT

133

"You can never move forward into the 'new' with an 'old' mind."

THOUGHT

134

"Pain is a powerful teacher. It makes sure its point is understood and its message heard loud and clear."

THOUGHT

135

"Seize the day with actions rather than complaints, and your day will be filled with what you can do instead of what you can't."

THOUGHT

136

"You can never hold in your hand what you don't first see in your mind."

THOUGHT

137

"Live to leave a legacy that will live even after you die and you will never die."

THOUGHT

138

*"Your life begins when you
discover the reason of your birth."*

THOUGHT

139

"I was over my past the moment God showed me that it worked together for my good."

THOUGHT

140

"People will never understand your grind until they witness your success."

THOUGHT

141

"Your tears water the garden in which your victory will sprout."

THOUGHT

142

"Greatness is often challenged by mediocrity."

THOUGHT

143

"Your words today are the seeds which contain your tomorrow's harvest. Plant with care, water with purpose, and you will reap with joy."

THOUGHT

144

"True champions view the ceiling as the floor."

THOUGHT

145

*"Don't let the morning wake you,
you awaken the morning!"*

THOUGHT

146

"A vision of victory is more powerful than any illusion of defeat."

THOUGHT

147

"Vision never stops speaking to those who are bold enough to listen."

THOUGHT

148

"Perfection is the result of corrected mistakes."

THOUGHT

149

"Live outside of the box that others may try to lock you within. Greatness knows no boundaries."

THOUGHT

150

"You are the best you there will ever be; but you absolutely suck at being someone else. Just be you."

THOUGHT

151

"It's okay to cry when you're going through but just don't become a cry baby"

THOUGHT

152

"You are worth more than you think."

THOUGHT

153

"Let no area of your life be off limits to the possibility of better."

THOUGHT

154

"When you have direction you don't wander aimlessly, but every step you take has purpose."

THOUGHT

155

"I discovered who I was when I realized who I wasn't."

Thoughts On
LOVE &
RELATIONSHIPS

THOUGHT

156

"Talk to him the way you would want him to speak to you. Be understanding of her the way you would want her to be understanding of you. Commit to resolve the issues and not abandon each other."

THOUGHT

157

"You cannot give less than 2% in a marriage but expect it to be 100% together. You will get out of it what you put into it."

THOUGHT

158

"He tried to love her, but she didn't love herself so she tore him down every chance she got just to make herself feel better. He wasn't perfect and they went through things, but he kept helping to make her a better person while she continued to tear him down. Eventually she murdered what love he did have for her."

THOUGHT

159

"Don't keep saying the same things over and over. Just start making changes and either they will get the clue and get right, or they will take a hint and get gone. Don't let your life be tied up begging people to be who and what they say they are to you. Keep it moving."

THOUGHT

160

"You are single until you're not. The only thing that doesn't make you single anymore is when you are engaged and then married. Boyfriends and girlfriends are not husbands and wives."

THOUGHT

161

"Sometimes it's best to simply wash your hands and walk away. You don't have to beg real love to love you."

THOUGHT

162

"There is nothing more toxic than a person who can never be accountable for their own actions but swears the issue is always everyone else."

THOUGHT

163

"Stop making excuses for people who continue to prove what they think of you by how they treat you; and stop tolerating the garbage of others in the name of love."

THOUGHT

164

"If some who is supposed to be in your corner can sing the praises of a stranger before they even offer you a kind and supportive word, they were never in your corner to begin with."

THOUGHT

165

"When she speaks her concerns don't dismiss them, and when he speaks his desires don't ignore them. You've got to listen to each other and adjust accordingly."

THOUGHT

166

"Never mistake those that benefit from being associated with you for those who genuinely support you."

THOUGHT

167

"Never put your relationship on auto pilot. A great relationship requires you to be in control even when things are out of control."

THOUGHT

168

"You want to know that he's going to be there and love you right 'no matter what'; and he wants to know the very same thing. But both of you need to clearly define the 'what' in the 'no matter what'."

THOUGHT

169

"Keep your single friends out of your married business."

THOUGHT

170

"You've got to be strong enough to love him past his mistakes, and you've got to be committed to loving her past her imperfections."

THOUGHT

171

"Don't let the fact that you loved the wrong one keep you from loving the right one. Don't punish the one you're with now because of the ones before."

THOUGHT

172

"If you couldn't play with certain kids as a child, you shouldn't hang with certain people as an adult. Watch your circle."

THOUGHT

173

"You apologizing doesn't mean the other person is right; it simply means that you are wise."

THOUGHT

174

"A woman, by design, is an incubator. You are designed to nurture, to care, to comfort and to provide strength. The right one can't come until you tap into what you were designed for. He needs you to function according to your design the same way you need him to."

THOUGHT

175

"A real man wants to build with you and not just build for you."

THOUGHT

176

"All he wanted was a woman who believed in him, and all she wanted was a man who made her feel secure. What she missed was that her security was directly connected to her believing in him. A good woman can make a great man."

THOUGHT

177

"Everyone wants to experience that moment when you look into another's eyes and realize that mentally, physically, and emotionally they have you...that you are theirs and they are yours...that you are in love."

THOUGHT

178

"The quality of your life can be found in the quality of the relationships you have."

THOUGHT

179

"You can't be there for everybody. Sometimes people have such a negative energy about them that it can literally suck all of the joy out of your atmosphere. For those type of people you have to learn to encourage them and keep moving. If you stay around them too long you will end up just like them."

THOUGHT

180

"Never beg a person to stay and never force a person to leave. Just keep moving forward and what will be will be. Just make sure you are prepared for whatever will be when it becomes."

THOUGHT

181

"Either it will work out or it won't. Don't get stuck trying to make a relationship work that just isn't working. Your happiness depends on you taking ownership of your relationships. Say 'goodbye' to that sadness so you can say 'hello' to joy."

THOUGHT

182

"The risk in loving is always better than the safety of the sidelines. You will miss life's greatest adventure being afraid to take the leap...to make the choice. I dare you to love."

THOUGHT

183

"Don't give up on love just because you've experienced the pain of loving boys who were pretending to be men, or because your heart was abandoned by little girls playing dress up in grown women's clothes...making them appear as something their consciousness had not yet caught up to. Don't give up on the one thing that has the power to give life. To give up on love is to give up on God and that would be a shame seeing that God hasn't given up on you. Don't give up on love."

THOUGHT

184

"The beauty of love is found in the risks love is willing to take. It's not in being cute, but it's in the risk of being ugly. It's not in being smart, but it's in the risk of looking like a fool. It's not in the certainty of outcomes, but it's in the risk of taking a leap of faith in the hopes that love will be the bridge that meets you at the other end of your leap. Love is a risk worth taking."

THOUGHT

185

"You will never have a healthy relationship, whether it be personal or professional, with someone who only wants to know you because of who and what you know."

THOUGHT

186

"Most treasures that are considered priceless today were discarded at some point by someone who didn't know the object's real worth. Don't let the fact that they discarded you make you doubt your worth. You are priceless."

THOUGHT

187

"Sex feels good, but sex with the right person is good. Don't get caught up in your feelings and mistake what feels good for what is good."

THOUGHT

188

"If he can't respect you with your clothes on then he should never see you with your clothes off. And if you're on the way to his house right now, stop and go back home."

THOUGHT

189

"Appreciate every laugh. Be grateful for every conversation. Cherish every kiss. Get lost in every lingering stare. Hang on each other's words. Live and love each other for life."

THOUGHT

190

"Dear Ladies, in your quest to be the baddest chic in the room, make sure you are also the smartest. A nice body alone is good for a show and late night rides, and will only attract kids who want to play; but it's the woman with the beauty and brains that gets a king."

THOUGHT

191

"Love yourself enough to love someone else. The power found in love is only unlocked when it's given away."

<u>THOUGHT</u>

192

"You and I could be the greatest love story, or we can be a pointless event."

THOUGHT

193

"After hearing a lot of words and seeing different actions, the only words you care to hear are the ones that match the actions."

THOUGHT

194

"Selfishness is a cancer that eats away at the fabric of any relationship. Marriages fall apart daily because of selfishness. My prayer is that we all learn to live selflessly."

THOUGHT

195

"Learn who is for you and who is against you. Give time to those who are for you and simply wave at those who are against you."

THOUGHT

196

"Don't allow people to hide behind titles in your life they have never lived up to."

THOUGHT

197

"Your inner circle cannot be filled with people who can never deliver."

THOUGHT

198

"There is nothing worse than constantly giving and getting absolutely nothing in return. You will eventually run empty and those that you were giving to will simply replace you when you can no longer give. For every relationship you have that takes from you, make sure you have at least two that pour back into you."

THOUGHT

199

"Rituals are the number one silent killers of relationships. You get so used to just going through the motions but your heart is not in it. Don't let your love be a ritual."

THOUGHT

200

"When there is no clear understanding relationships are strained and often broken because everyone is operating off of what they think instead of what's supposed to be."

THOUGHT

201

"Lies comfort the one who tells them, but they destroy the ones who they are told to."

THOUGHT

202

"When dealing with difficult people, remembering everything you are will help you deal with everything they're not."

THOUGHT

203

"Effective communication prevents future misunderstandings."

THOUGHT

204

"People who always want to be understood but can never understand are weights."

THOUGHT

205

*"The problem is not that you feel
what you feel, but it's that you
force how you feel on others."*

THOUGHT

206

"It's not that I'm trying to avoid you, it's just that we are going in opposite directions."

THOUGHT

207

"They should be able to see you in your weakness and speak strength."

THOUGHT

208

"If you cannot trust them with your flaws then they are not worthy of your last name."

THOUGHT

209

"The true test of if someone really loves you is how they treat you when others can't see. The true test of if you really love someone is if you operate right even when they operate wrong."

THOUGHT

210

"Every day gives you the opportunity to love better than you did the day before. Let love grow."

THOUGHT

211

"Pick your battles wisely. Every difference isn't worth a discussion."

THOUGHT

212

"Find the joy in making each other happy. Doing this will strengthen your relationship with one another."

THOUGHT

213

"If everyone around you is always in need of a hookup and at the end you're footing the bill; it's time to change the people around you quick."

THOUGHT

214

"People with no focus will always try to break your focus with mess which should never be a focus. Surround yourself with focused people."

THOUGHT

215

"You can either build him up or tear him down, but always remember that your conversation is fertilizer in the ground of your relationship."

ACKNOWLEDGEMENTS

To all of my friends, family, and associates, thank you for the roles that you play in my life. I don't take any of you for granted.

ABOUT THE AUTHOR

Fred T. Williams is an Author, Speaker, Life Coach, Entrepreneur, and Brand Strategist. Originally from Monroe, Louisiana, currently residing in Chicago, Illinois, Fred is a rising voice on faith, purposeful living, healthy relationships, love, and brand development. Fred travels the world sharing a message of hope and tenacity. He has assisted organizations and entrepreneurs in establishing a memorable presence amongst their target audience. Fred has helped many unlock the greatness within them, while enabling them to find their passion, live their purpose, and gain the cutting edge in life.

=

<u>Visit Fred online:</u>

www.fredtwilliams.com

<u>Connect with Fred on Social Media:</u>

Facebook/Instagram: @fredtwilliams
Twitter/Periscope: @fredtwilliams1

If you would like to hire Fred as your Life
Coach, please visit www.fredtwilliams.com and
click on the appropriate links.